About Love and sexual energy

Tatyana N. Mickushina

UDC 141.339=111=03.161.1
BBC 87.7+86.4
   M 59

M 59 Mickushina, T.N.
About Love and sexual energy /
T. N. Mickushina. – 2017. – 90 pages.

This book tells us about the most elevated feeling of
Love – Divine Love.

This book also contains the forgotten ancient
knowledge on the use of sexual energy, which by
following this advice you can improve your own health
and that of your family as well as facilitate prosperity
and well-being.

This book is intended for the attention of a broad
reading audience.

ISBN-10: 1540700194
ISBN-13: 978-1540700193

Contents

From the author

This book, offered to readers' attention, is a revised version of my previously published book, You love, it means you are alive! This new book is intended for a broad reading audience. The book is based on the Messages of the Masters of Wisdom, which were being recorded by me during the period of 2005-2015. The Messages are available on the "Sirius" website: **sirius-eng.net** or in the series of books *Words of Wisdom*.

Divine Love and earthly love. What is the difference between them?

Is sex love? Think about whether the degradation of moral standards that exists in our society is harmless. How can a person become a source of the perfect feeling of Love?

The reader will get the answers to these and many other questions when reading the Words of Wisdom contained in this book.

Tatyana N. Mickushina

Cultivate the feeling of Love in your heart.

Your foremost task in life is to regain the feeling of Love at any price.

All is God. And your separation from the Unity with God is only in your consciousness.

You love, and it means you are alive! And that is the chief thing.

**Open your hearts
to Divine Love
and you will change
this world**

The quality of Love is the greatest of all the Divine qualities. The aspiration to love, the desire to love and to be loved is characteristic of all living creatures. It is exactly due to the breach of the Divine Law, which happened due to the abuse of free will that the greatest distortions were brought into this quality.

If we managed to completely restore this quality in the souls of just a few people embodied now, we would disseminate it around the world very quickly. This is a quality impossible to oppose.

This is a quality that allows you to tune into the Divine Reality immediately.

Very often, this quality is mixed up with the sexual instinct. Hence, different sexual perversions take place.

The human talent for creative work and the creative power of people are manifested through Love. The creative power, which is the basis of the conception of a child, is at the same time the basis of everything created by Man in his life.

Man is inherently similar to God. The keynote quality of God is Love. Thus, it is impossible for Man not to create.

However, the creative power can be manifested only as much as it is not limited by blocks of anti-love inculcated into Man's consciousness from outside and supported by his imperfect consciousness from within.

The Perfect Flame of Love comes to this world through Man's energetic system. But filters of people's imperfect thoughts and feelings are in the path of this stream of Love. As a result, the stream is distorted. You are constantly showing the quality of Divine Love. It is impossible for you not to show this quality because it is inherent in all creation. You should simply purge the filters from both your consciousness and your perception of the Divine Reality.

Open your hearts to Love, Divine Love, and you will change this world.

There is no force mightier than Love in this world.

Therefore, those forces that have decided to separate from God, first of all, parasitize on the distortions of the quality of Divine Love.

The entire industry of sex and pornography, stereotypes of interrelations between the sexes propagandized and circulated by mass media, are aimed at keeping you from any manifestation of Divine Love.

It seems harmless if you watch a film cultivating your desire to satisfy your sexual instinct. It seems to be an innocent amusement to look at a naked female body advertising subjects that are absolutely unnecessary for your spiritual development.

As a result, hatred for Divine Love settles in your consciousness. You voluntarily strengthen the filters embedded in your consciousness, which prevent you from the manifestation of the true Love quality in your life.

It is impossible to draw a comparison between the primordial Divine manifestation of Love and the understanding of love that has settled in the mass consciousness of people.

It is like life and death.

One of the qualities of the saints is their ability to absorb the nectar of Divine Grace into their hearts. There is no pleasure in this physical world that can be compared to receiving this Divine Grace.

Only pure hearts are capable of obtaining this Grace.

A stream of Divine energy and Divine Love passes through all your bodies and caresses you. You experience ecstasy in every chakra, in every energetic center.

The greatest sexual satisfaction that you can have in the physical life cannot be compared with the experience of the Grace sent to you by God.

Think about whether it is harmless for you to watch pornographic films, to tolerate foul language, to be in the company of people admitting dirty thoughts and conduct in their attitude toward women and sexual interrelations.

Each of such negative vibrations contributes to your separation from the quality of Divine Love.

Contemplate flowers, nature, and children's smiles. Constantly guard your love against any manifestations of anti-love. Guard your relatives and your children. The future of your planet depends on the conception of Love, which will be obtained by the new generation.

The True Love begins with the veneration of a woman, a Mother. The feelings you experience toward your mother can leave their mark on your whole life. The happiest families are those where the respect for the Mother, as the keeper of the hearth, has become a tradition.

May your consciousness never be burdened with any bad thoughts directed against Mother, against the female source.

I wish for you to acquire the quality of Divine Love in your lives.

Cultivate the feeling of Love in your heart

Love is the most essential of all the Divine qualities.

Whole worlds are created by Love. And if you do not feel joyfulness in your life, if you are weighed down by heavy thoughts and feelings, you just lack Love within your being.

It does not matter whether you are loved or not. Love is a force that lives deep inside of you. And it is always with you as long as you receive the Divine Energy from its Source.

That is why a mere deficiency of this feeling of Love brings you into a discordant state of consciousness. The quality of Love runs through the entire Creation and is organically involved in your life and the lives of all living creatures.

Many problems in the world, if not to say all the problems of this world, are directly connected with the deficiency of Love.

Here is some advice on how to anchor the focus of Love within your heart.

You may perform this exercise every day when you have a free minute. This exercise requires neither special preparation nor additional conditions. You may perform it at home or at work, among people in the busiest places.

Thus, you should always see in your mind's eye the image of a person you love. I understand very well that many of you may say that you do not feel love toward anybody in this world. This is a delusion. You must love. You must find in your consciousness an image toward which you feel love.

It does not have to be an image of your beloved. However, you can search your soul attentively and try to find the image toward which you are able to feel love.

This can be your mother, your father, your spouse, or your children.

If your heart suffers from a trauma so severely that the very reminder of your beloved causes self-pity and tears in your eyes, you should still look for an image toward which you could aspire with your consciousness and toward which you could feel Love.

It could even be your pet or favorite plants.

Cultivate the feeling of Love in your heart.

Your foremost task in life is to regain the feeling of Love at any price.

If you are surrounded by people, try to feel love toward them. Love people not for something they have done or can do for you, just feel unconditional Love.

Maybe you will not be able to concentrate on your feeling of Love for long. Nevertheless, you should find at least two or three minutes a day to experience this feeling of Love.

Cultivate this feeling inside of you.

And the day will come when you will be able to experience a strong, all-consuming and causeless feeling of Love for everything surrounding you, for all people living on Earth, for the very Earth, for nature, clouds, sky, rain, and sun.

You will be overwhelmed with the feelings of Love and Unity with everything surrounding you. But you are all this simultaneously. Try to understand that your consciousness, your human consciousness, separates you from the surrounding world and that your human nature and the nature of everything around you are alike.

All is God. And your separation from the Unity with God is only in your consciousness.

I still appeal to you to experience more often the feeling of Love for all the living. It is only Love that is capable of performing miracles in your life and in the lives of the people surrounding you.

You love, and it means you are alive! And that is the chief thing.

All you need is to be inspired with love tAll you need is to be inspired with love toward the whole life, to any manifestation of life, and feel your Oneness with every part of life.

Let the Divine energy flow through your being freely; and on its way it will wash away all small and big obstacles in the form of your ego, your fears, limits, and dogmata.

Joy and Love. It is enough for you to cultivate only these two qualities within yourselves, and you will see how everything will start changing in your life.

A Teaching
on the energy
of the Divine
Mother

Love, the quality of Love, True Love, the Divine Love, is catastrophically lacking in the world now.

The worlds are created by Love, and the worlds collapse due to the lack of the quality of Love. It is time for you to think about Love and its manifestations in your life in real earnest.

In reality, the heart chakra, which passes the energies of Love into the physical world, is completely blocked in the majority of people. Therefore, you are short of Love, and you try to compensate for its shortage by strange practices stimulating a pure physiological instinct. Trust me; the majority of distortions of the Divine Energy in the physical world are connected exactly with the misuse of the energy of the Divine Mother or, in other words, your sexual energy.

God endowed you with the Sacred Fire, the Flame of the Sacred Fire, which makes you similar to Gods. And this flame and this energy were given to you, not for your pleasure. The more thoughtlessly you use your Sacred Fire, the more karma you create. Mass media, the stereotypes of behavior in modern society, and even your way of behaving and dressing stimulate the misuse of your sexual energy.

In the course of time, you will be able to understand the authentic intention of the Sacred Fire granted to you by God.

But now you ought to understand that every time you use this gift, not in accordance with the Divine intention, you create karma. You create karma as you waste the Divine Energy for receiving shallow and purely animal pleasures. However, animals act much more reasonably than you in this respect. Their use of sexual energy happens at least in the framework of yearly cycles at an appropriate season of the year.

During an act of sexual intercourse, a gigantic amount of the Divine Energy is released. This release of the Divine Energy can be compared to a flash of a supernova. You know that your energy flows in exactly the same direction as your attention. And if at the moment of release of the Divine Energy, you think of receiving pleasure for yourself and your partner, you use your sexual energy wrongly. Many of you will find these words impossible to absorb into your consciousness. I am absolutely aware that my words will sound strange to many of you. But you must understand the very elementary basis of the Divine Ethics, which are known, even to animals, but have been forgotten by mankind for some reason.

Everything in this world belongs to God. You are particles of God. Therefore, everything you do, all your actions must conform to the Divine Law and take place within the framework of this Law. If you do something against the Will of God, you violate the Law of this universe and create karma.

Thus, no matter how strange these instructions and recommendations seem to you, please simply listen to them from the beginning.

Before an act of sexual intercourse, please bring your actions into line with the Will of God. You must be in lawful wedlock with your sexual partner. You must never have homosexual intercourse or sexual intercourse with accidental partners.

Why is it so necessary to be in lawful wedlock with a constant partner?

The point is that while performing your matrimonial duty, a direct exchange of energy between your partner and you takes place. Communicating with people, you constantly exchange energies, but your energy exchange during sexual intercourse is multiplied greatly. In fact, you exchange all your energies – both good ones and bad ones. You take upon yourselves the karma of each other, and you share your merits with your sexual partners. If you are in lawful wedlock, then during your mutual life you have an opportunity to work out not only your own karma but also the karma of your spouse, if the latter outbalances yours.

Now imagine that you are engaged in sexual intercourse with many partners. And imagine that the percentage of the karma they have worked out is much less than yours. Their karmic loads can be much heavier than yours. They might have come to this world to work out their karma of murder, betrayal, or some other dire kinds of karma. When you absolutely thoughtlessly have sexual intercourse with them, you take upon yourself a part of their karma. And if at the same time you are in lawful wedlock, you take this karma upon your family. So, how can you be shocked when all your life problems crop up after that?

Sexual energy has the same nature as the energy used for creation in the physical world. And when you waste your sexual potential for pleasure, you deprive yourself of creative energy and limit your evolution. In reality, such an abuse of sexual energy results in the absolute incapability of the majority of people for higher creative activity because they are too devastated when they approach maturity. They are simply incapable of becoming co-creators with God and of performing any creative work.

It is exactly through the abuse of the energy of the Divine Mother that the greatest part of the energy is distorted by mankind.

Every act of intercourse within wedlock should be performed in the name of God. Pray to God and dedicate the Sacred Fire released during your sexual intercourse to God. Remember that your energy flows in exactly the same direction as your attention. And if you dedicate the release of your Sacred Fire to God, you will direct all the freed energy into the higher spheres of Light. And this energy will return to you afterward as blessings for you and your children.

Try to use the Energy of the Divine Mother only for the aim of conceiving children. If at first it is difficult for you to be confined to such limitations, try to cut down the number of your acts of intercourse to once or twice a week.

Do not forget to direct all the released energy to God at least in an unspoken wish. Ask God to use this energy for blessing you, your children, and your whole family.

Always remember that all your actions in the physical plane can be used for both good and evil. Every minute and every second of your life in the physical world, you receive the Divine Energy, and you either direct it for the creation of the illusion — when it forms a sediment in this world and multiplies the illusion — or you send it toward the Divine world, creating good karma and multiplying your treasures and merits in Heaven.

The use of your sexual energy should be the cornerstone of your life.

The True Love begins with the veneration of a woman, a Mother.

The feelings you experience toward your mother can leave their mark on your whole life.

The happiest families are those where the respect for the Mother, as the keeper of the hearth, has become a tradition.

A Teaching on Love and life trials

If a miracle occurred and all the people began to experience the feeling of Love, an instantaneous miracle of transformation would happen. Love is the quality that this world is constantly lacking. However, in reality, Love is the quality that is inherent in this world primordially. Your constant feeling of the shortage of Love is evidence of the fact that you are following a wrong Path.

If only you could continually experience this beautiful all-embracing feeling! In this case, your mind and your emotional body could be in an elevated state all the time, and you would be able to keep your vibrations continually on the highest level available for you.

But what else do you need?

When a man becomes filled with high vibrations, when he is full of the feeling of Divine Love, he feels a causeless state of happiness and his life becomes full of sense, concord, and harmony.

The quality that is called "love" by the majority of humans on Earth has, in fact, nothing in common with the true Love, Pure Love — Divine Love.

It can be said with a feeling of full certainty and trustworthiness that the true feeling of Love is as big of a rarity in your world as your meeting with the Angels.

If you were able to raise your vibrations up to the feeling of Divine Love at least for a very short time, you would manage to commune with the Higher World almost instantaneously.

The Angels are very responsive to the quality of Love.

In many Teachings given through many messengers, it was said that Love is a key. Do you understand now why Love is a key?

It is because this feeling is able to raise your vibrations instantaneously and to approximate them to the vibrations of the etheric octaves of Light. And you become able to come into contact with the Higher World based on the feeling of the Divine Love.

This feeling of Love, True Love, Divine Love, when being experienced by you, is a signal of your readiness to communicate with the Divine world. This very feeling of Love creates for you an absolutely impenetrable defense from the attacks of any negative forces and energies and from any individuals who have submitted themselves to the actions of these negative forces.

That is why it is very easy to identify the direction of your movement. If you experience a feeling of causeless Love, joy, and peace, then you are moving in the right direction. You are ready to

29

embrace the entire world, and you are ready to give help to the whole planet.

You are seized by causeless generosity, happiness, and a wish to give out more and more of your Light and your Love, to grant your Love to the world, and to ask for nothing in exchange.

On the contrary, if you have lost your way and are going in the wrong direction, you feel a deficiency of Love and, as a consequence of this, suspicion, fear, and condemnation. Any person filled with Love will differ so much from you by his vibrations that you will feel irritation toward him.

You see that the criterion of the faultlessness of your Path is very simple.

You either experience the feeling of Love, or you do not have it.

But as long as only a very small percent of the people of Earth can feel this noble feeling, you can form an opinion about the number of people who are moving in the right direction.

Love, the quality of Love, True Love, the Divine Love – is catastrophically lacking in the world now.

The worlds are created by Love, and the worlds collapse due to the lack of the quality of Love. It is time you should think about Love and its manifestations in your life in real earnest.

The success of your
evolution on this
beautiful planet
depends on the
development of
the quality of Divine
Love in you

———— ⊙⊱⊰⊙ ————

Everything in this universe is based on the great power of Love, and everything that there is in this universe exists only due to the power of Love.

Love is the essence of this universe. Therefore, your vibrations are solely the vibrations of Love when they are as close to the vibrations of the universe as possible. The more you are able to manifest the quality of Love in your heart, the closer you get to the true reality, and move away from your physical illusion. However, there is a big difference between the shades of the quality of Love in the physical world and in the Higher World. What many of you mean by Love is, in fact, not Love at all. The feeling that you sometimes call love is equal to the sexual instinct or the instinct of sex, and there is no difference between that feeling and the one that the birds and animals have. Therefore, first of all, you should think about the quality of the Love you experience.

True love has no attachment at all to a definite sex or to the object of Love. This is an inner feeling, having no attachment to a definite being or an object; it is Love toward everyone, toward the whole of creation, the whole of Life, and the whole universe.

Many of you, being in nature, can raise your vibrations to the true feeling of Love.

But the power and the fullness of that Love can be even more intense. Your physical bodies simply cannot experience the loftier and finer manifestations of this amazing quality of Love. Each of you shows love in your own way, and each of you has your own inherent individual and personal understanding of the quality of love.

At the beginning of Creation, God divided his Love into an infinite number of parts, and each of you, being a part of God, received your own little part of Love. Now you have an opportunity to experience that Love and to refine it. That is why you have to get rid of everything in your life that prevents your feeling of Love from growing.

Observe your lives thoroughly, and try to trace the states you experience most often. You will be surprised that you hardly ever experience the feeling of Love, which is inherent in the whole of Creation, the true feeling of Love. And even when the time of your first love comes, it is very seldom that this feeling is not colored with a possessive instinct and the desire to own the object of your love. Therefore, the success of your evolution on this beautiful planet depends on the development of the quality of Divine Love within you.

No matter how you resist, you do not have a choice, and sooner or later you will follow the path destined for you by the plan of the great Creator of this Universe.

And that is the path of the highest Love and the highest bliss. Everything that separates you from that state is subject to gradual refusal and must leave your consciousness and your lives, for such is the Law. You have to make your own choice and follow this Law — the Law of the highest and unconditional Love.

Now it is hard for you to believe that everything around you is just the manifestation of the non-divine feeling of anti-love. Yes, everything you have created, which is not based on the great feeling of Love, will disappear in the course of time and will stop existing. What will be left is what is perfect in God, which is primarily the feeling of Divine unconditional Love not shadowed by human consciousness.

It seems to you that you have made great achievements, but all of your achievements are directed at multiplying the illusion. At the current stage, other achievements are required of you: the achievements in the field of developing the Divine quality within you, with Divine Love as the main quality. Yet there are other qualities that you have to develop in yourselves.

Faith and Love are two sisters, two loving sisters, who are inseparable in eternity. There is also Hope. Hope alone can unfold your consciousness when it seems to you that there is no way out of the deadlock and disorder of the storms of life.

With every successive cycle of evolution, you will get closer and closer to the Divine Reality, and it will become easier for you. In the course of time the awareness of this reality will come, and happiness will overflow in you and will never leave you. The twilight of your consciousness is coming to an end. The new dawn and the awakening in the new reality are ahead.

Guidance for
every day

All knowledge and understanding comes with the feeling of deep unconditional Love.

Only based on the feelings of Divine Love are you able to comprehend the Truth. This is the law that works unalterably when the energy is being exchanged between the octaves. When you experience fear, doubt, and other imperfect feelings, you will be unable to comprehend the whole goodness of the Divine Truth. On the other hand, if you are able to cultivate this feeling of unconditional Divine Love, you will be able to see tremendous Truth, even in one single phrase. This phrase will mean nothing to the majority of mankind, but for you it will open up the whole fullness of the Divine Truth because you have received the key to open it, namely the Divine Love in your heart. Therefore, do not strive to cultivate the pursuit of knowledge within yourselves, but strive to cultivate the pursuit of the Divine Love. Your perfection in God is not possible if you cannot develop the quality of Divine Love within yourselves.

You cannot imagine how quickly and clearly mankind will begin to advance on the Divine Path if you are able to understand the importance of the all-encompassing feeling of Love. Many, if not all the tests on your Path can be overcome only with the feeling of Love. When the Divine Love leaves you, it can be compared to a severe illness. Nobody will help you with that illness if you do not desire to return to the elevated state of consciousness and to the feeling of all-encompassing Love. The feeling of unconditional Love is what you lack; it is what will be the best remedy for you on the spiritual Path.

It is impossible to feel Love if you are driven by other imperfect feelings. For example, the feeling of fear occurs due to the shortage of Love. You are afraid to lose something or you are afraid that someone will harm you, but the mere reason why you have these fears is because you do not have Love in your heart. Therefore, the best remedy for fear will be Love, the Love that is Divine in its nature. If you experience Love that is not Divine, then that imperfect feeling can make you attached to the object of your affection. You should feel the unconditional Love that is not related to a particular person and which is more general. You should love each being in your world and each being in the Divine world.

When you see too many imperfections in other people, it also means that you experience the shortage of Love. You cannot notice imperfections and feel Love at the same time. These are incompatible qualities.

In the beginning, it will be difficult for you to experience the feeling of unconditional Love because

41

your understanding of love is related to human sentiments too much. Therefore, do not be ashamed if, in the beginning, your love is not perfect.

The strength of your Love is also important because Love is the quality that allows you to act in your world. Strength without Love turns into craftiness and resentment. Therefore, you need to start and do everything in your lives only with the feeling of Love. If you have any personal motive, it makes all your actions imperfect. When you try to do a good deed only with your mind, without hearing the sound of the Divine feeling of Love within you, your deed may lead to a bad result instead of a good outcome.

Remember what Jesus taught you: "By their fruits, you will recognize them.[1]"

Your actions may be absolutely correct; you may be praying, doing community service, helping others, but no matter what you do, it will lead to poor results. This happens because, at the moment when you decided to do something, your intention was not colored with Love. Thus, the fruit, the result of your actions, was rotten. Therefore, it is better to do nothing instead of starting something without the feeling of Love because the karma, as the result of your actions, will be negative in this case.

---

[1] By their fruits you will recognize them (Mathew 7:16).
For a good tree brings not forth corrupt fruit; neither does a corrupt tree bring forth good fruit, for every tree is known by his own fruit (Luke 6:43-44).

Do you understand how the Law of karma works? Do you understand what more and more subtle aspects of this Law open up to you as you advance on your Path?

Let us make the analogy of an educational institution. When you first go to school, you go to the first grade, and then you transfer to the second and third grades. Only very arrogant people go straight to the ninth grade and demand to study there. Knowledge cannot fill the vessel if the vessel is not prepared properly. That is why very difficult Truths are given in very simple words. Many people become deluded by that. It seems to them that everything discussed are old truths.

Allow me to note that in this case you are driven by your ego, and the lack of the Divine Love will play an evil trick on you someday. That is why the Teaching is given based on the feeling of deep unconditional Love, but you also need to accept the nectar of the Teaching when you are attuned to the Divine tone and filled with Love. It is recommended that you do not begin reading until you reach a balanced state of consciousness.

It is important for you to pay attention to every small detail that surrounds you in your life. You should maintain tidiness in your house, at your workplace; you should carefully select the food you eat and maintain the cleanliness of your body. Note to yourself that in addition to the physical dirt, you also collect a lot of astral and mental dirt throughout the day. The best way of cleaning yourself from that dirt will be bathing in a pure natural reservoir or at least taking a shower or a full bath twice daily, in the morning and in the evening.

You Love.

No matter how you hide your Love or pretend that you do not remember your Love, it is still present within you. Your primary quality is Love.

Remove all unnecessary things from your life that impede you from feeling the Divine Love in your heart.

Only with the feeling of unconditional, endless Love are you able to build true relationships in your world

Jesus visited the Earth 2000 years ago. One of the aims of His coming was to give the humanity of Earth an example of Love — not of the Love based on the fleshly desire but of the Love based on a more elevated Divine feeling.

Jesus was speaking about it, and Jesus was teaching his students about the relations founded on this feeling of Love. The relations based on the mutual feelings of Love are the only and necessary condition when a community (several people or families) gathers to live together.

It is difficult for you to understand this feeling that one feels toward all people without exception. However, Jesus had this gift. God gave Him this ability: to Love all people. It is thanks to this ability that He was able to withstand all the ordeals God sent to Him.

Only with the feeling of unconditional, endless Love are you able to build true relations in your world.

You are used to feeling love toward your parents, to men and women, and to children. All of these are different manifestations of one and the same Divine Love, but these are only small manifestations, narrow ones. There is greater Love, the Love that does not differentiate between men, women, children, animals, and even things of inanimate nature.

There is Love that expands boundlessly and includes the whole Creation, everything that surrounds you.

It is very hard to feel such Love in your world. However, if you do not learn to Love in this way, then you will not be able to move along the Path of evolutionary development.

In every one of you there is a particle of God that is not manifested, and the task for each of you is to manifest God, to give God the opportunity to act through you.

Now you are too preoccupied and anxious about your worldly affairs. You are constantly in a bustle and toiling over the fulfillment of big and small tasks of life. The time will come when you will be able to discern more global pictures of the development of the human civilization behind the whole fuss of life. You will learn to watch and see how in every life situation that arises before your sight, the causes, which you alone have created earlier, come into action. You will learn to distinguish causes from effects. Gradually you will be able to unravel the tapestry of Life and to see the reality that exists behind it. You will be able to discern the real world of God.

For now, you have much to learn, and you are yet to understand many things.

God is Love

Never chase external rituals. Never try to find sacraments where there are none. Live simply. Follow the commandments given by Moses and the prophets and, first and foremost, try to maintain in your heart the feelings of Love and compassion toward your neighbors and all living beings.

The way you treat every particle of Life, the way you treat any Divine manifestation, will distinguish a true believer from a hypocrite who covers up with the name of God but does not have God in his heart.

Jesus had given the commandment "Love each other." When Love lives in your heart, you do not need any external preacher; you do not need to spend your time searching for God outside of yourselves because you have Love and, therefore, you reside in God because God is Love.

Every person living in the physical world has a right to be loved.

"Love thy neighbor as thyself." It was so long ago that this commandment was given by beloved Jesus. So many events have taken place on the Earth since the time of this commandment.

How busy you are in your lives! You are constantly busy with something. Is it not the time to stop and hear Jesus' words addressed to you?

You should treat
your children as if
the Angel of God
has come to you
as your child

Look at your children. The faces of many of them resemble the faces of great wise men. Look into their eyes. A newborn baby comes from the Higher World. He remembers the Divine world. And what does he see around him? He sees the fuss. He sees a mess and a lot of noise. But he does not see that you wish to accept him as God and that you wish to know the secret he came to tell the world.

In the first months of his life, a child is dwelling within our world by half or even less. At this time you have a lot to learn from him. Of course, he cannot teach you with words or actions. But he can pass on to you the state of the Divine world. This state is in his aura. Many people intuitively try to touch a child, pick him up in their arms or pat him on his head. These automatic actions certainly allow you to come in touch with the Higher World through the child.

But you have forgotten that your child is the messenger of the Divine world, and you have indulged in your usual occupation. You watch TV, talk on the phone, and listen to music. You wonder why your child is restless, why he often cries and is capricious.

But what you do differs so much from the Divine world that a child is just under continual stress. He cannot tell you to turn off your music or your TV; he cannot ask you to stop talking on the phone. He shows displeasure with all of this with his tears and thereby shows you that he does not want to hear all that. You think that a child wants to eat or drink, or that he has just gotten tired and wants to sleep.

Your attitude toward your children needs to be reconsidered. You should treat your children as if the Angel of God has come to you as your child.

In His presence would you do all the things that you do in the presence of your child, thinking that he understands nothing?

Would you behave in the way that you behave?

In the first months of life, a child's aura can be as large as a whole city. You truly meet the messenger of the Heavens. But do you do all necessary things in order to meet the messenger of the Heavens?

You think that your children understand nothing.

You think they are silly and cannot perceive reality as you see it.

Children come into your world having the image of the other world. Many of them are wise souls who have passed the earthly school of initiations. And what do they see? They see parents and relatives using "baby talk." And no one in the whole world treats them as wise souls who know everything since their birth.

The aura of a baby gradually absorbs the environment of the family, the city, and the country in which he was born, and by the age of three, a child loses the memory of the Higher World. He absorbs your habits, your attachments, and the stereotypes of your behavior. By the age of three, a child's aura is burdened with all the negative states that you have had, and that you still have. And if he can watch TV or listen to the radio when you think he is asleep or understands nothing, then a child is imbued with the whole nightmare that flows like a river from your mass media. And who you see in front of you as three years old is not an angel having come into your world, but a soul burdened with all the sins of the world, a soul who will have to work off the karma of the family, the karma of their kin, the karma of the country, and the karma of the world until the end of his earthly life.

You must have careful attitudes — and not only to children. Every person living in the physical world has a right to be loved.

"Love thy neighbor as thyself." It was so long ago that this commandment was given by beloved Jesus. So many events have taken place on the Earth since the time of this commandment. How busy you are in your lives. You are constantly busy with something. Is it not the time to stop and hear Jesus' words addressed to you?

How many times is it necessary to repeat the commandments so that they are followed?

Contemplate flowers, nature, and children's smiles. Constantly guard your love against any manifestations of anti-love.

Guard your relatives and your children. The future of your planet depends on the conception of Love, which will be obtained by the new generation.

A Teaching on the liberation from negative energies

---- ❧ ----

This talk is about where your psychological problems come from and whether it is possible for you to free yourselves from them without resorting to human psychotherapists. It should be said that the spiritual Teachers and the human psychotherapists approach the liberation from psychological problems differently. Human psychotherapists use the terms "subconsciousness" and "unconscious," whereas the spiritual Teachers usually use the terms "soul" and "subtle bodies."

There would be no big difference in it if the specialists approached you not as a client and a source of their subsistence in the physical world but as a soul that needs help and support.

The deplorable fact is that practically all the people living on planet Earth now are in need of help. It means help in solving psychological problems that are burdening your souls and pass from embodiment to embodiment. Many specialists and psychotherapists reject the fact that the soul has a very ancient history and passes through many incarnations. And this makes it impossible to fully help many of the souls who need help. Many problems can come to you from your previous embodiments, for example, various fears, phobias, or traumatic deaths. Many souls are burdened with these problems and do not know how to free themselves from them.

There is no universal prescription. Only some recommendations can be given.

First of all, it is necessary to realize the problem that is within you and burdens your subtle bodies, for example, hatred toward the opposite sex which came from your past. You have a beautiful family in your current embodiment, and there is no cause for the manifestation of hatred and enmity. But you can do nothing with yourself. From time to time you experience attacks of hatred and anger. You yourself suffer from them, and your nearest and dearest — your spouse, your children — suffer from them too.

The first and the main step to the solution of your problem is the recognition that this problem exists within you. This is a very big and vital step. When you are reading these lines, it may seem funny to you that it is possible not to recognize such a problem. Do not jump to conclusions. You can see this problem in other people, but when the karmic energy of hatred and enmity rises within you, when it overwhelms you and totally flows over you like an ocean wave, you cannot evaluate the situation rationally. Your anger seems to you fully justified, and you find, or rather your carnal mind finds, a thousand satisfactory excuses for your state, your behavior, and your actions.

When this horrible negative energy from your past embodiments rises within you, it is very difficult for you to cope with yourself. You do not know how many times in your past incarnations you experienced the most severe treatment from the opposite sex. You could have been humiliated, beaten up, and even violated and killed. The records of all these negative experiences are lying in your subtle bodies as a burden. And your task, your foremost task, is to try to realize that this energy, this negative energy, is present within you.

It is not your husband or wife that is the cause of your negative state of consciousness, but the energy that exists within you. The difficulty of the situation is that more than likely within your husband or wife there is also an energy that needs to be worked off. And most probably, if under the influence of the negative energy you blame your husband, for example, for some actions or thoughts that he does not have in the current embodiment, then exactly in his previous embodiments, he acted precisely in the way that that you chastise him for. Therefore, the process of healing from the low-quality energies becomes more complicated because this is a mutual process. You yourselves can render help to each other to free yourselves from the negative energies. You just need to agree between yourselves that when this negative energy is rising in one of you, the other must signal that here it is, this energy has risen. And then, helping each other, you will become aware of the presence of this energy in you. And you will be able to separate this energy from yourself.

You will become able to realize that this is the very part of you that you wish to free yourself from.

The second vital step comes when you recognize the presence of the negative energy that exists within you and you begin to feel an impulse to get rid of it.

The next step is the simplest one. You ask God to liberate you from the negative energy that is present within you. But with all its seeming simplicity, this step cannot be done by everybody. As a rule, people's consciousness is very mobile. They are able to ask God once or twice to free them from the negative energy, but then they forget about their appeal, about their decision to get rid of the negative energy. When the next karmic moment comes and the negative energy totally flows over them again, people are puzzled about why God didn't free them from this energy.

This, beloved, is because the negative energy that is present within you has sometimes been formed during the whole previous embodiment and at times even during several embodiments. That is why you should go to great lengths in order to become free from this energy.

Sometimes only your everyday endeavors during a number of years are able to help you to free yourself from the negative energies of the past.

The negative qualities that you acquire during the current embodiment are worked off much more easily, but the qualities that accompany you from embodiment to embodiment take a lot of effort to be worked off.

And many qualities can be worked off through direct interaction with your spouses. Day after day, facing each other's negative qualities, you realize that these are the negative energies that you need to free yourself from, and you forgive each other and help each other during your whole lives.

Only this way, by helping each other, are you sometimes able to overcome the karma of the past. And the main element that is able to help you in dissolving the past karma is the love that you feel toward each other. It is the greatest treasure of your world which is worth cherishing and protecting much more than money, things, or gold.

Love is the most essential of all the Divine qualities.

Whole worlds are created by Love. And if you do not feel joyfulness in your life, if you are weighed down by heavy thoughts and feelings, then you just lack Love within your being.

It does not matter whether you are loved or not. Love is a force that lives deep inside of you. And it is always with you as long as you receive the Divine Energy from its Source.

A Teaching on
the correct use of
sexual energy

Your Kundalini energy, or the energy of the Divine Mother, or sexual energy is asleep in the chakra at the base of the spine.

We touch upon a Teaching that will make many of you take another look at your sexual desires. The purpose of this instruction is to protect those souls, who are able to hear the message, from falling lower by misusing their sexual energy.

What new things can be said, and what is the best way to instruct you on what would not be known to mankind many hundreds and thousands of years ago? Modern culture ignores many things that are so natural and have been passed on from generation to generation for thousands of years. This is a Teaching on the correct use of sexual energy. It is exactly your attitude toward your inner power and your sexual potential that determines your further evolutionary path.

When you are able to use your sexual energy reasonably, you subdue the animal part of yourself, and so you approach being the Divine human. The subject of this talk can appall many of you because your actions in the past were not so perfect. Every time you thoughtlessly and unnecessarily waste your Divine potential, you create karma. Your creative power, your creative ability, and your health depend directly on your ability to control your sexual energy.

Society does not provide a detailed explanation on this subject in school education or in educating future parents. However, this important subject is to engross your mind, and when you begin to think over this theme, there is a probability that you will be able to properly dispose of your sexual energy in future.

Sexual energy depends directly on your creative power, on your ability to create in any sphere of human activity. It follows as a conclusion that a careful, especially careful, attitude toward this kind of energy is required.

You may not agree and state the fact that the energy is given by God and so the source of this energy is unlimited.

This is true, but on the condition that you have mastered the right attitude toward this kind of energy. Why do you think so many miracles of materialization, teleportation, and other miracles are impossible in your time? One reason is that the flow of the Divine energy into your body is closed to its maximum. You do not have access to the Divine energy even to the extent that was possible just a few thousand years ago. The flow of the Divine energy is being closed even more, as more and more of humanity falls into ignorance.

You think ignorance means that you cannot use a TV, computer, or cell phone. No, ignorance is that you do not follow the Divine Law that exists in this universe. One of the points that this Law states is about the necessity to carefully use sexual energy.

Each person possesses a certain potential. And this potential can be depleted prematurely. In this case you will become a hollow man, a man without God within himself. Your eyes are dying, so you become the living dead in the course of your earthly life.

Sexual culture is to be the part of the general culture of society. The events we witness now are the stage of dissolution of morals in society, as it was in the days of Sodom and Gomorrah. You may have heard what happened to these cities.

All people are at different stages of evolutionary development. There are a very small percentage of people who, since their births, are capable of using the Divine energy in the right way. In essence, these people are very great incarnations or they are partial incarnations. Other people are able to control their sexual energy and keep it within certain bounds. But for this, they must be aware of what the consequences of the superfluous waste of sexual energy are. All stereotypes of behavior in society and mass culture are not conducive to the creation of the right patterns in this field. Therefore, it is necessary to have the inner and conscious resistance to your temptations.

In any case, this precious energy must not be used for pleasure. It would be perfect to use this energy only for conceiving children.

We have talked about two categories of people who can fully or partially control their sexual energy.

Unfortunately, the rest of the people have fallen even lower than animals because what is allowed in mass media and on the Internet cannot be described by any other words but the absolute dissolution of morals.

The lightest energy, which makes people similar to Gods, has been associated in the minds of humanity with debauchery and something unclean.

Your minds must be put to order. You must separate the Divine from what is evil in this subject. You must separate the wheat from the chaff in this matter because the greatest distortion of the Divine energy in the world is connected exactly with all kinds of sexual distortions.

You can start your
service exactly
where you are
at this moment

Many bright souls are thinking about an opportunity to improve the surrounding life, about an opportunity to serve people.

There are certain expectations in people's minds concerning their possible service to Life. It is necessary to clear up this point. You don't need to wait until you receive some opportunities, money, power, or a post at your disposal.

When you need something in order to start your service, apart from what you already have, you act according to your carnal mind's prompt. The only thing you need to start your service to people is your desire. And nothing else is needed.

You can start your service exactly where you are at this moment. Everything you are doing now can be directed by you for the service to Life. Look, what are you doing now?

You are at home and you are busy with your household duties. It's beautiful! You are already serving Life!

How can it be that you clean the house or wash the dishes and so you are serving Life? The point is in the way you are doing it. Any even the smallest and most insignificant task that you do in your lives can be done with great Love. If you perform small deeds with great Love, thinking about how your family and your closest ones will be happy when they enter their clean home and put on their clothes, snow-white and just washed by you, then you are already serving Life. Your service can be manifested in every task. If you do your work very carefully and with Love, then any kind of activity transforms the space there. When your children or your husband come home tired and burdened from a hectic day, the atmosphere of Love that you created at home can transform their hearts and restore harmony in their souls.

It is very difficult to maintain inner balance and the feeling of Love when you are at work because not all the people who you see during the day are harmonious and friendly. You more often face imperfect manifestations of human consciousness. That is where a wide field is open for you, for your action and your service. You must master the skill of neutralizing any negativity using Love, patience, and humility. You are given so many opportunities in your life to manifest your service! Almost every task, every meeting, everything that happens to you during the day can be used to fulfill your service. Only when you learn to find the points in which you can apply your soul's best qualities in everyday activities and in the details of life, and when none of the outer problems can break your inner peace and harmony, only then will the other opportunity for your service appear. And you will be able to use the qualities that you have already developed in the new stage of your service to people, which is inseparable from Service to Life.

Many of you seek the help of God and ask to be given an opportunity for your service, to be given an opportunity to prove yourself in service. Are you honest with yourself? God has already taken care of everything. You already have the best conditions to start your service and to work on your qualities that prevent you from manifesting Love and care to your neighbors in the most difficult life situations. Until you learn to see great service in the little nothings of life, you will not be able to progress along the Path of evolution. Look, what do you really wish? Do you wish to be a dignitary or to manage something, or do you really wish to serve?

The answer to this question will determine your whole life. You will either struggle to the end of your life to take up a post or to prove to someone that you already have great spiritual attainments, or you will serve without attracting any outside attention and do God's deeds on Earth, and subsequently on a much larger scale.

The aim of this talk is to give you an understanding of the difference between true service and false service. Yes, as everything in this world has two sides, likewise, service has two different sides.

Each time, before you start doing something, think about what you are being driven by. Is it a desire to prove something to others, to show your greatness or to show everyone your diligence? Are you driven by Love for your neighbor, which is inherent in you and affects everything you do? Very simple things that you perform selflessly with great unconditional Love remain with you forever as the treasures of your causal body. Your earthly life will be over but your attitude toward your deeds and toward people will remain and will accompany you in your next incarnation.

The world lacks so much for the quality of true service to Life, the service to mankind of the Earth.

These are simple truths. Probably, you already know all this or you have read or heard of it.

Yet, let me ask you, "What prevents you from applying this knowledge in your lives?"

There is sometimes an abyss between something that you know or have read or heard of and the real application of this knowledge in your lives.

You need to think more about what prevents you from manifesting Divine qualities in your life and gradually, step by step, get rid of everything that impedes you.

Do not think that your attitude toward work, people, plants, or animals goes unnoticed if there are no witnesses of your good deeds or actions. Everything is recorded in the Akashic Records: every action, thought, feeling, and deed, both negative and positive. Think it over and go through your life with care, leaving no astral or mental garbage.

May all your progress along your life only be accompanied by Love and the fragrance of roses!

Only with the feeling of unconditional, endless Love are you able to build true relations in your world.

Love people not for something they have done or can do for you, just feel unconditional Love.

Open your hearts to Love, Divine Love, and you will change this world.

There is no force mightier than Love in this world.

You are creating
your own future
and the future of
the whole planet
at the moment
of conception
of your child

Let us speak about the concerns that are very near and understandable for everybody. And more particularly, we are going to speak about your future, about your children, and about the generation of people that will take your place.

By human standards, a short period of time will pass, and a new generation of people will take the place of the generation that is living now. And each successive generation should be better than the previous one. However, it does not always happen. Why? Perhaps, many of you wondered why your children do not resemble you. Why are they impudent, disobedient, and guided in their lives by completely different principles from those you were guided by in your time? What is the reason for that?

We will probably approach this subject from a standpoint unusual to you. Remember the period that preceded the time of your child's birth. There is no need to share that memory with anybody. Just try to recollect — how it happened that a baby was born to you.

Perhaps, you will remember that you came to find out that you would have a baby. You might even have been sad or vexed at that fact.

Maybe you had not even planned to have a baby, and yet he emerged.

What were you thinking about when enjoying carnal pleasures with your partner? Most of you almost certainly were not thinking about creating a new human being, who was to come to this world and become a creator of this world.

Your energy flows where your attention is directed. Were you thinking about getting pleasure for yourself or for your sex partner? The precious Divine energy was directed at getting pleasure.

But the Divine Will played a trick on you, and a baby appeared. What did your child get in such a case? What part of the Divine energy?

You yourselves disposed of the Divine energy and directed it to getting pleasure. In this case, what from that precious energy did a new being receive, who was aspiring to your world so much?

You supplied your child with only the residual amount of the Divine energy. That is, the entire Divine energy boost that was to be granted to your child for all his life remained on the things around you when you were seeking pleasures.

Now you remember that moment.

Some of you may say that you were expecting a baby and praying for its birth. And indeed, your child was long-expected and welcomed by you. But remember those days of your youth that preceded your child's birth.

You wanted to get sexual pleasures; you experimented with your sexual energy. You used to do many things that you are even ashamed to remember. And every time you got pleasure, you were wasting your sexual potential that was required for your child's birth in order for your child to be healthy not only physically but also mentally. And when you settled down and were looking forward to the conception of your long-expected firstborn, do you think he got much of the Divine energy? Didn't you supply your child only with the residual amount?

If your sexual pleasures were wild and indecent, what soul do you think you can attract as your child? Everything is attracted according to vibrations, and the soul you will attract as your firstborn will be attracted after you have burdened yourself with a significant amount of karma that was accumulated while satisfying your desires.

After your consideration, haven't you come to realize that you yourselves are to blame for all the problems of the next generation of people on planet Earth?

You cannot say that you have nothing to do with the fact that each new generation is less and less viable than the previous one.

So, in order to change the situation on the planet, you should be clearly aware of the connection between all your actions and the consequences to which your actions lead.

Only then, when you learn to control your desires, thoughts, and feelings, will you be able to gradually overcome the karma of your past wrong choices and deeds.

You should be warned about another mistake. Many of you are inclined to blame yourselves for the improper deeds that you performed in your youth. And sometimes this feeling of guilt gives rise to a whole complex of psychological problems. Instead of strengthening your focus on your child and family in order to correct your mistakes of the past, you plunge into depression and even start feeling fear of the Divine scourge.

God does not want to punish you. He wants you to realize your mistakes and not to repeat them in the future. There is no sinner without a future. And sometimes a man who has realized his mistakes and repented of them can do much more for mankind than a person who does not do anything improper out of fear of the Divine scourge.

Do direct your energy to a positive path! Do not dwell on the scenes of your past sins and mistakes over and over again. That will only make matters worse because you will be directing your energy to the same wrong path. The river of the Divine energy that flows through you should find a new channel for itself and wash away the consequences of all the wrong states of consciousness of the past.

Constant concentration on the positive and on a desire to help the beings around you and, primarily, your children, can transform the energy of past mistakes and create a new opportunity for the future of your children.

Complete realization of past mistakes and a fervent desire not to repeat them are quite enough to change the karmic consequences and create a better tomorrow for your children.

Do not forget that you have created karmic connections with your children. And there is a strong probability that in your future incarnations you will be the children of those individuals who are your children now. In order to alleviate your karma in the future, you should, first of all, be concerned about your children's souls now.

Everything is interconnected in the world, and it is necessary to treat everything you do thoughtfully and with due care.

The purpose of the talk today was to give you the knowledge about the importance of a thoughtful approach to planning a child's birth. In fact, you are creating your own future and the future of the whole planet at the moment of conception of your child. Think of that next time when satisfying your sexual desire.

Tatyana N. Mickushina

About Love
and sexual energy

Buy Books by Tatyana N. Mickushina on Amazon:
amazon.com/author/tatyana_mickushina

Websites:
http://sirius-eng.net/ (English version)
http://sirius-ru.net/ or http://sirius-net.org
(Russian version)

Cover image from the site kira-scrap.ru

CPSIA information can be obtained
at www.ICGtesting.com
Printed in the USA
BVHW040832100920
588537BV00010B/180

9 781540 700193